My Character Journal For

_____

(Working Title)

A Fiction Writer's Character Workbook

Created by

KIMBERLY BLACK

For the Soon-to-be-Bestselling Author:

_____

Steepledog Productions

ISBN: 150103023X
ISBN-13: 978-1501030239

DEDICATION

To all the amazing characters I have met in my life.

*In writing, a good guy must never
break any of the
Ten Commandments.
A bad guy must break every one.
That's why writing female characters is
so much fun.
They're not guys at all.*

Dear Writer Friend,

I designed this workbook as a tool for developing the characters for the story already growing in your imagination. My hope is that through the process of pouring out the details of your beloved (and sometimes despised) characters, you will be better able to make them as real to your readers as they are to you.

This exercise is also a great method for keeping track of details that have a way of slipping through the cracks between chapters, and managing characters that may travel through a whole series of stories.

I have included "prompts" that may or may not be relevant to your plot. Use them or change them to suit your cast of characters. Always remember to vary your players' backgrounds to add depth and realism to your story.

This workbook includes sections for up to 15 Character Studies.

Best wishes for success,
Kimberly Black

CHARACTER NAME: _____

Sketch or Inspiration Photo:

Character Type: __ Main   __ Major   __ Minor   __ Protagonist __ Antagonist

Nickname/Alias: _____

Age/Birthdate: _____

Height: _____ Weight: _____

Build/Body Type: _____

Hair Color/ Type: _____

Eye Color/ Type: _____

Occupation: _____

Education: _____

Skills/ Talents: _____

_____

Relationship Status: _____

Love Interest(s): _____

Vehicle/ Transportation: _____

Personal Style: _____

_____

Parents' Names: _____

Relationship: _____

Siblings: _____

Relationship: _____

Other Family: _____

Past Friends: _____

Catchphrase: _____

Life Philosophy/ World View: _____

_____

_____

Main Goal: _____

_____

_____

Character Secrets: _____

_____

_____

Motivating Factors: _____

_____

This character would NEVER: _____

_____

(The best characters are often forced to do the one thing they would never willingly do

Five Facts that ABSOLUTELY MUST BE INCLUDED in the Story:

1. _____

2. _____

3. _____

4. _____

5. _____

(TIP: Hi-light these facts as they appear in your manuscript.)

Miscellaneous: _____

_____

_____

_____

_____

History/ Bio: _____

_____

_____

_____

_____

_____

_____

_____

_____

_____

_____

_____

_____

_____

Continued :_____

_____

_____

_____

_____

_____

_____

_____

_____

_____

_____

_____

_____

_____

_____

_____

_____

CHARACTER NAME: _____

Sketch or Inspiration Photo:

Character Type: __ Main   __ Major   __ Minor   __ Protagonist   __ Antagonist

Nickname/Alias: _____

Age/Birthdate: _____

Height: _____   Weight: _____

Build/Body Type: _____

Hair Color/ Type: _____

Eye Color/ Type: _____

Occupation: _____

Education: _____

Skills/ Talents: _____

_____

Relationship Status: _____

Love Interest(s):   _____

Vehicle/ Transportation: _____

Personal Style: _____

_____

Parents' Names: _____

Relationship: _____

Siblings: _____

Relationship: _____

Other Family: _____

Past Friends: _____

Catchphrase: _____

Life Philosophy/ World View: _____

_____

_____

Main Goal: _____

_____ _____

_____

Character Secrets: _____

_____

_____

Motivating Factors: _____

_____

This character would NEVER: _____

_____

(What's the big deal if they do it?)

Five Facts that ABSOLUTELY MUST BE INCLUDED in the Story:

1. _____

2. _____

3. _____

4. _____

5. _____

(TIP: Hi-light these facts as they appear in your manuscript.)

Miscellaneous: _____

_____

_____

_____

_____

History/ Bio: _____

_____

_____

_____

_____

_____

_____

_____

_____

_____

_____

_____

_____

_____

Continued : _____

_____

_____

_____

_____

_____

_____

_____

_____

_____

_____

_____

_____

_____

_____

_____

_____

_____

CHARACTER NAME: _____

Sketch or Inspiration Photo:

Character Type: __ Main   __ Major   __ Minor   __ Protagonist __ Antagonist

Nickname/Alias: _____

Age/Birthdate: _____

Height: _____   Weight: _____

Build/Body Type: _____

Hair Color/ Type: _____

Eye Color/ Type: _____

Occupation: _____

Education: _____

Skills/ Talents: _____

                   _____

Relationship Status: _____

Love Interest(s): _____

Vehicle/ Transportation: _____

Personal Style: _____

                   _____

Parents' Names: _____

Relationship: _____

Siblings: _____

Relationship: _____

Other Family: _____

Past Friends: _____

Catchphrase: _____

Life Philosophy/ World View: _____

_____

_____

Main Goal: _____

_____ _____

_____

Character Secrets: _____

_____

_____

Motivating Factors: _____

_____

This character would NEVER: _____

_____

(Who would this action most affect?)

Five Facts that ABSOLUTELY MUST BE INCLUDED in the Story:

1. _____

2. _____

3. _____

4. _____

5. _____

(TIP: Hi-light these facts as they appear in your manuscript.)

Miscellaneous: _____

_____

_____

_____

_____

History/ Bio: _____

_____

_____

_____

_____

_____

_____

_____

_____

_____

_____

_____

_____

Continued :_____

_____

_____

_____

_____

_____

_____

_____

_____

_____

_____

_____

_____

_____

_____

_____

_____

CHARACTER NAME: _____

Sketch or Inspiration Photo:

Character Type: __ Main __ Major __ Minor __ Protagonist __ Antagonist

Nickname/Alias: _____

Age/Birthdate: _____

Height: _____ Weight: _____

Build/Body Type: _____

Hair Color/ Type: _____

Eye Color/ Type: _____

Occupation: _____

Education: _____

Skills/ Talents: _____

_____

Relationship Status: _____

Love Interest(s): _____

Vehicle/ Transportation: _____

Personal Style: _____

_____

Parents' Names: _____

Relationship: _____

Siblings: _____

Relationship: _____

Other Family: _____

Past Friends: _____

Catchphrase: _____

Life Philosophy/ World View: _____

_____

_____

Main Goal: _____

_____ _____

_____

Character Secrets: _____

_____

_____

Motivating Factors: _____

_____

This character would NEVER: _____

_____

(Why not?)

Five Facts that ABSOLUTELY MUST BE INCLUDED in the Story:

1. _____

2. _____

3. _____

4. _____

5. _____

(TIP: Hi-light these facts as they appear in your manuscript.)

Miscellaneous: _____

_____

_____

_____

_____

History/ Bio: _____

_____

_____

_____

_____

_____

_____

_____

_____

_____

_____

_____

_____

Continued :_____

CHARACTER NAME: _____

Sketch or Inspiration Photo:

Character Type: __ Main   __ Major   __ Minor   __ Protagonist __ Antagonist

Nickname/Alias: _____

Age/Birthdate: _____

Height: _____ Weight: _____

Build/Body Type: _____

Hair Color/ Type: _____

Eye Color/ Type: _____

Occupation: _____

Education: _____

Skills/ Talents: _____

_____

Relationship Status: _____

Love Interest(s): _____

Vehicle/ Transportation: _____

Personal Style: _____

_____

Parents' Names: _____

Relationship: _____

Siblings: _____

Relationship: _____

Other Family: _____

Past Friends: _____

Catchphrase: _____

Life Philosophy/ World View: _____

_____

_____

Main Goal: _____

_____

_____

Character Secrets: _____

_____

_____

Motivating Factors: _____

_____

This character would NEVER: _____

_____

(In what circumstances would this be a reasonable option for this character?)

Five Facts that ABSOLUTELY MUST BE INCLUDED in the Story:

1. _____

2. _____

3. _____

4. _____

5. _____

(TIP: Hi-light these facts as they appear in your manuscript.)

Miscellaneous: _____

_____

_____

_____

_____

History/ Bio: _____

_____

_____

_____

_____

_____

_____

_____

_____

_____

_____

_____

_____

Continued :_____

_____

_____

_____

_____

_____

_____

_____

_____

_____

_____

_____

_____

_____

_____

_____

_____

CHARACTER NAME: _____

Sketch or Inspiration Photo:

Character Type: __ Main   __ Major   __ Minor   __ Protagonist __ Antagonist

Nickname/Alias: _____

Age/Birthdate: _____

Height: _____   Weight: _____

Build/Body Type: _____

Hair Color/ Type: _____

Eye Color/ Type: _____

Occupation: _____

Education: _____

Skills/ Talents: _____

_____

Relationship Status: _____

Love Interest(s): _____

Vehicle/ Transportation: _____

Personal Style: _____

_____

Parents' Names: _____

Relationship: _____

Siblings: _____

Relationship: _____

Other Family: _____

Past Friends: _____

Catchphrase: _____

Life Philosophy/ World View: _____

_____

_____

Main Goal: _____

_____ ____

_____

Character Secrets: _____

_____

_____

Motivating Factors: _____

_____

This character would NEVER: _____

_____

(Who would be most disappointed if they did?)

Five Facts that ABSOLUTELY MUST BE INCLUDED in the Story:

1. _____

2. _____

3. _____

4. _____

5. _____

(TIP: Hi-light these facts as they appear in your manuscript.)

Miscellaneous: _____

_____

_____

_____

_____

History/ Bio: _____

_____

_____

_____

_____

_____

_____

_____

_____

_____

_____

_____

_____

Continued :_____

_____

_____

_____

_____

_____

_____

_____

_____

_____

_____

_____

_____

_____

_____

_____

_____

_____

CHARACTER NAME: _____

Sketch or Inspiration Photo:

Character Type: __ Main   __ Major   __ Minor   __ Protagonist __ Antagonist

Nickname/Alias: _____

Age/Birthdate: _____

Height: _____   Weight: _____

Build/Body Type: _____

Hair Color/ Type: _____

Eye Color/ Type: _____

Occupation: _____

Education: _____

Skills/ Talents: _____

_____

Relationship Status: _____

Love Interest(s):   _____

Vehicle/ Transportation: _____

Personal Style: _____

_____

Parents' Names: _____

Relationship: _____

Siblings: _____

Relationship: _____

Other Family: _____

Past Friends: _____

Catchphrase: _____

Life Philosophy/ World View: _____

_____

_____

Main Goal: _____

_____

_____

Character Secrets: _____

_____

_____

Motivating Factors: _____

_____

This character would NEVER: _____

_____

(Is there any way to make this okay?)

Five Facts that ABSOLUTELY MUST BE INCLUDED in the Story:

    1. _____

    2. _____

    3. _____

    4. _____

    5. _____

(TIP: Hi-light these facts as they appear in your manuscript.)

Miscellaneous: _____

_____

_____

_____

History/ Bio: _____

_____

_____

_____

_____

_____

_____

_____

_____

_____

_____

_____

_____

Continued :_____

_____

_____

_____

_____

_____

_____

_____

_____

_____

_____

_____

_____

_____

_____

_____

_____

_____

CHARACTER NAME: _____

Sketch or Inspiration Photo:

Character Type: __ Main   __ Major   __ Minor   __ Protagonist __ Antagonist

Nickname/Alias: _____

Age/Birthdate: _____

Height: _____   Weight: _____

Build/Body Type: _____

Hair Color/ Type: _____

Eye Color/ Type: _____

Occupation: _____

Education: _____

Skills/ Talents: _____

_____

Relationship Status: _____

Love Interest(s):   _____

Vehicle/ Transportation: _____

Personal Style: _____

_____

Parents' Names: _____

Relationship: _____

Siblings: _____

Relationship: _____

Other Family: _____

Past Friends: _____

Catchphrase: _____

Life Philosophy/ World View: _____

_____

_____

Main Goal: _____

_____ _____

_____

Character Secrets: _____

_____

_____

Motivating Factors: _____

_____

This character would NEVER: _____

_____

(Would they do it to save someone else's life?)

Five Facts that ABSOLUTELY MUST BE INCLUDED in the Story:

1. _____

2. _____

3. _____

4. _____

5. _____

(TIP: Hi-light these facts as they appear in your manuscript.)

Miscellaneous: _____

_____

_____

_____

_____

History/ Bio: _____

_____

_____

_____

_____

_____

_____

_____

_____

_____

_____

_____

_____

_____

Continued :_____

_____

_____

_____

_____

_____

_____

_____

_____

_____

_____

_____

_____

_____

_____

_____

_____

CHARACTER NAME: _____

Sketch or Inspiration Photo:

Character Type: __ Main   __ Major   __ Minor   __ Protagonist __ Antagonist

Nickname/Alias: _____

Age/Birthdate: _____

Height: _____   Weight: _____

Build/Body Type: _____

Hair Color/ Type: _____

Eye Color/ Type: _____

Occupation: _____

Education: _____

Skills/ Talents: _____

_____

Relationship Status: _____

Love Interest(s):   _____

Vehicle/ Transportation: _____

Personal Style: _____

_____

Parents' Names: _____

Relationship: _____

Siblings: _____

Relationship: _____

Other Family: _____

Past Friends: _____

Catchphrase: _____

Life Philosophy/ World View: _____

_____

_____

Main Goal: _____

_____

_____

Character Secrets: _____

_____

_____

Motivating Factors: _____

_____

This character would NEVER: _____

_____

(What's the worst thing that could happen?)

Five Facts that ABSOLUTELY MUST BE INCLUDED in the Story:

     1. _____

     2. _____

     3. _____

     4. _____

     5. _____

(TIP: Hi-light these facts as they appear in your manuscript.)

Miscellaneous: _____

_____

_____

_____

_____

History/ Bio: _____

_____

_____

_____

_____

_____

_____

_____

_____

_____

_____

_____

_____

Continued :_____

_____

_____

_____

_____

_____

_____

_____

_____

_____

_____

_____

_____

_____

_____

_____

_____

_____

CHARACTER NAME: _____

Sketch or Inspiration Photo:

Character Type: __ Main   __ Major   __ Minor   __ Protagonist __ Antagonist

Nickname/Alias: _____

Age/Birthdate: _____

Height: _____   Weight: _____

Build/Body Type: _____

Hair Color/ Type: _____

Eye Color/ Type: _____

Occupation: _____

Education: _____

Skills/ Talents: _____

_____

Relationship Status: _____

Love Interest(s): _____

Vehicle/ Transportation: _____

Personal Style: _____

_____

Parents' Names: _____

Relationship: _____

Siblings: _____

Relationship: _____

Other Family: _____

Past Friends: _____

Catchphrase: _____

Life Philosophy/ World View: _____

_____

_____

Main Goal: _____

_____

_____

Character Secrets: _____

_____

_____

Motivating Factors: _____

_____

This character would NEVER: _____

_____

(Would doing this make the story more interesting?)

Five Facts that ABSOLUTELY MUST BE INCLUDED in the Story:

1. _____

2. _____

3. _____

4. _____

5. _____

(TIP: Hi-light these facts as they appear in your manuscript.)

Miscellaneous: _____

_____

_____

_____

_____

History/ Bio: _____

_____

_____

_____

_____

_____

_____

_____

_____

_____

_____

_____

_____

Continued :_____

_____

_____

_____

_____

_____

_____

_____

_____

_____

_____

_____

_____

_____

_____

_____

_____

CHARACTER NAME: _____

Sketch or Inspiration Photo:

Character Type: __ Main   __ Major   __ Minor   __ Protagonist __ Antagonist

Nickname/Alias: _____

Age/Birthdate: _____

Height: _____   Weight: _____

Build/Body Type: _____

Hair Color/ Type: _____

Eye Color/ Type: _____

Occupation: _____

Education: _____

Skills/ Talents: _____

                    _____

Relationship Status: _____

Love Interest(s):   _____

Vehicle/ Transportation: _____

Personal Style: _____

                    _____

Parents' Names: _____

Relationship: _____

Siblings: _____

Relationship: _____

Other Family: _____

Past Friends: _____

Catchphrase: _____

Life Philosophy/ World View: _____

_____

_____

Main Goal: _____

_____ _____

_____

Character Secrets: _____

_____

_____

Motivating Factors: _____

_____

This character would NEVER: _____

_____

(Could including this be an effective plot twist?)

Five Facts that ABSOLUTELY MUST BE INCLUDED in the Story:

     1. _____

     2. _____

     3. _____

     4. _____

     5. _____

(TIP: Hi-light these facts as they appear in your manuscript.)

Miscellaneous: _____

_____

_____

_____

_____

History/ Bio: _____

_____

_____

_____

_____

_____

_____

_____

_____

_____

_____

_____

_____

_____

Continued :_____

_____

_____

_____

_____

_____

_____

_____

_____

_____

_____

_____

_____

_____

_____

_____

_____

_____

_____

CHARACTER NAME: _____

Sketch or Inspiration Photo:

Character Type: __ Main   __ Major   __ Minor   __ Protagonist __ Antagonist

Nickname/Alias: _____

Age/Birthdate: _____

Height: _____   Weight: _____

Build/Body Type: _____

Hair Color/ Type: _____

Eye Color/ Type: _____

Occupation: _____

Education: _____

Skills/ Talents: _____

_____

Relationship Status: _____

Love Interest(s):   _____

Vehicle/ Transportation: _____

Personal Style: _____

_____

Parents' Names: _____

Relationship: _____

Siblings: _____

Relationship: _____

Other Family: _____

Past Friends: _____

Catchphrase: _____

Life Philosophy/ World View: _____

_____

_____

Main Goal: _____

_____ _____

_____

Character Secrets: _____

_____

_____

Motivating Factors: _____

_____

This character would NEVER: _____

_____

(Would you do it?)

Five Facts that ABSOLUTELY MUST BE INCLUDED in the Story:

1. _____

2. _____

3. _____

4. _____

5. _____

(TIP: Hi-light these facts as they appear in your manuscript.)

Miscellaneous: _____

_____

_____

_____

_____

History/ Bio: _____

_____

_____

_____

_____

_____

_____

_____

_____

_____

_____

_____

_____

_____

Continued :_____

_____

_____

_____

_____

_____

_____

_____

_____

_____

_____

_____

_____

_____

_____

_____

_____

_____

_____

CHARACTER NAME: _____

Sketch or Inspiration Photo:

Character Type: __ Main   __ Major   __ Minor   __ Protagonist __ Antagonist

Nickname/Alias: _____

Age/Birthdate: _____

Height: _____   Weight: _____

Build/Body Type: _____

Hair Color/ Type: _____

Eye Color/ Type: _____

Occupation: _____

Education: _____

Skills/ Talents: _____

                    _____

Relationship Status: _____

Love Interest(s):   _____

Vehicle/ Transportation: _____

Personal Style: _____

                    _____

Parents' Names: _____

Relationship: _____

Siblings: _____

Relationship: _____

Other Family: _____

Past Friends: _____

Catchphrase: _____

Life Philosophy/ World View: _____

_____

_____

Main Goal: _____

_____

_____

Character Secrets: _____

_____

_____

Motivating Factors: _____

_____

This character would NEVER: _____

_____

(Go ahead and do it.)

Five Facts that ABSOLUTELY MUST BE INCLUDED in the Story:

1. _____

2. _____

3. _____

4. _____

5. _____

(TIP: Hi-light these facts as they appear in your manuscript.)

Miscellaneous: _____

_____

_____

_____

_____

History/ Bio: _____

_____

_____

_____

_____

_____

_____

_____

_____

_____

_____

_____

_____

Continued :_____

_____

_____

_____

_____

_____

_____

_____

_____

_____

_____

_____

_____

_____

_____

_____

_____

_____

_____

CHARACTER NAME: _____

Sketch or Inspiration Photo:

Character Type: __ Main   __ Major   __ Minor   __ Protagonist __ Antagonist

Nickname/Alias: _____

Age/Birthdate: _____

Height: _____   Weight: _____

Build/Body Type: _____

Hair Color/ Type: _____

Eye Color/ Type: _____

Occupation: _____

Education: _____

Skills/ Talents: _____

_____

Relationship Status: _____

Love Interest(s):   _____

Vehicle/ Transportation: _____

Personal Style: _____

_____

Parents' Names: _____

Relationship: _____

Siblings: _____

Relationship: _____

Other Family: _____

Past Friends: _____

Catchphrase: _____

Life Philosophy/ World View: _____

_____

_____

Main Goal: _____

_____

_____

Character Secrets: _____

_____

_____

Motivating Factors: _____

_____

This character would NEVER: _____

_____

(And where would be the most inappropriate place to do it?)

Five Facts that ABSOLUTELY MUST BE INCLUDED in the Story:

1. _____

2. _____

3. _____

4. _____

5. _____

(TIP: Hi-light these facts as they appear in your manuscript.)

Miscellaneous: _____

_____

_____

_____

_____

History/ Bio: _____

_____

_____

_____

_____

_____

_____

_____

_____

_____

_____

_____

_____

Continued :_____

_____

_____

_____

_____

_____

_____

_____

_____

_____

_____

_____

_____

_____

_____

_____

_____

CHARACTER NAME: _____

Sketch or Inspiration Photo:

Character Type: __ Main   __ Major   __ Minor   __ Protagonist __ Antagonist

Nickname/Alias: _____

Age/Birthdate: _____

Height: _____ Weight: _____

Build/Body Type: _____

Hair Color/ Type: _____

Eye Color/ Type: _____

Occupation: _____

Education: _____

Skills/ Talents: _____

_____

Relationship Status: _____

Love Interest(s): _____

Vehicle/ Transportation: _____

Personal Style: _____

_____

Parents' Names: _____

Relationship: _____

Siblings: _____

Relationship: _____

Other Family: _____

Past Friends: _____

Catchphrase: _____

Life Philosophy/ World View: _____

_____

_____

Main Goal: _____

_____ _____

_____

Character Secrets: _____

_____

_____

Motivating Factors: _____

_____

This character would NEVER: _____

_____

(What are the consequences?)

Five Facts that ABSOLUTELY MUST BE INCLUDED in the Story:

1. _____

2. _____

3. _____

4. _____

5. _____

(TIP: Hi-light these facts as they appear in your manuscript.)

Miscellaneous: _____

_____

_____

_____

_____

History/ Bio: _____

_____

_____

_____

_____

_____

_____

_____

_____

_____

_____

_____

_____

_____

Continued :_____

_____

_____

_____

_____

_____

_____

_____

_____

_____

_____

_____

_____

_____

_____

_____

_____

_____

_____

ABOUT THE AUTHOR

Kimberly Black is an award-winning author, designer, and blogger. She works from her hometown in the Texas Panhandle and enjoys spending time with her family and friends.

OTHER TITLES BY KIMBERLY BLACK

Pockets
© 2013/2014
Steepledog Productions
available in kindle and paperback

Lydia, Woman of Purple
© 2014
Buoy Up Press
available in kindle and paperback